Venison Recipes Made Simple

99 Classic Recipes for the Homecook

GEORGE T. GREGORY

Venison Recipes Made Simple

99 Recipes for the Homecook

ISBN-10: 1-940253-02-0
ISBN-13: 978-1-940253-02-2

Printed and bound in the United States of America
First Printing: September 2013

Author: George T. Gregory

Publisher: Stonebriar Books - StonebriarBooks.com

Book and Cover Design: Samantha Gardner

First Edition

Contents

INTRODUCTION

I was twelve years old when I shot my first whitetail deer. I was so excited. That excitement turned to disappointment when my mother slapped a deer steak in a frying pan and cooked it till it was almost black. It was so tough that what I was able to chew tasted terrible.

Unfortunately, my experience has been the same for countless individuals who have tasted poorly prepared venison for the first time and vowed never to try it again.

My saving grace was a neighbor who was a hunter with a great collection of venison recipes. After hearing my tale of woe, he was gracious enough to share a few simple ground venison recipes that even my mother couldn't destroy.

Thank you Mr. Dean.

Over the next fifty plus years, I have accumulated my own treasure chest of recipes, which I have decided to share in this book. Included are the preparation of ground venison, steaks, tenderloins and roasts. Enjoy!

ABOUT THE AUTHOR

A lifelong outdoorsman, George grew up and continues to reside in Pennsylvania, a state rich in deer hunting tradition. He has been fishing and hunting all types of game since an early age. However, deer hunting has always been his passion, both with a rifle and with a bow.

It has always been important to George never to waste any of the meat from the deer he has taken, so over the years he has found many different ways to prepare venison.

He is also the author of the best selling *Freshwater Fish Recipes Made Simple.*

George is passing his love of hunting and fishing onto his three grandsons – *Landen, Lucas and Jack.*

Chapter 1

Roasts

Basic Venison Roast

Enjoy this simple to prepare roast recipe.

Serves: 6

Preparation Time: 5 Minutes

Cooking Time: 4 Hours

Ingredients:
- 3 pound venison roast
- 2 teaspoons salt
- 1 teaspoon pepper
- 1 onion, peeled and thinly sliced

Preparation:
1. Place roast in a heavy frying pan or Dutch oven and set to medium temperature. Brown thoroughly on all sides.
2. Sprinkle with salt and pepper. Place onion slices on top.
3. Cover and cook over low heat for 4 Hours or until done.

George's Most Simple Venison Roast

Here's a way to make a roast that is simple and never fails.

Serves : 6

Preparation Time: 5 Minutes

Cooking Time: 8 Hours

Ingredients:
- 3 pound venison roast
- 1 package dry onion soup mix
- ¼ cup water
- ⅛ teaspoon black pepper

Preparation:
1. Mix ingredients and pour over roast in crock pot.
2. Cook on low for 8 Hours or until tender.

Crockpot Venison Roast

This roast will get your taste buds excited.

Serves: 10

Preparation Time: 20 Minutes

Cooking Time: 8 Hours

Ingredients:
- 3 pound venison roast
- 1 can cream of mushroom soup
- 1 cup dry red wine
- 2 beef bouillon cubes
- 2 garlic cloves, minced
- 1 tablespoon Italian seasoning
- 2 teaspoons thyme leaves
- 1 tablespoon Tabasco sauce
- 1 onion, chopped
- 1 can (8 ounces) sliced mushrooms
- 8 potatoes, cubed
- 6 carrots, peeled and cut into 2 inch long pieces

Preparation:
1. Mix all ingredients (except for roast) in a large bowl until well blended.
2. Place roast in crockpot and pour mixture over roast.
3. Cook on low for 8 to 10 Hours or until done.

Dad's Venison Roast

The extra marinating time makes this recipe worth the effort.

Serves: 6

Preparation Time: 20 Minutes (Needs additional 24 Hours of marinating time)

Cooking Time: 3-4 Hours

Ingredients:
- 3 pound venison roast
- 4 cups white vinegar
- 4 cups water
- 4 tablespoons salt
- 8 cloves
- 1 pound beef suet
- 1 pound bacon
- Salt, to taste
- Pepper, to taste

Preparation:
1. Place roast in pan. Poke knife holes over entire surface of roast.
2. Pour water and vinegar over roast until completely covered. Add additional liquid if necessary. Add cloves and let sit for 24 Hours.
3. Remove roast from pan and rinse with water.
4. Press thin strips of suet and bacon in the knife holes in the roast and salt and pepper to taste.
5. Place any remaining bacon or suet on top of the roast.
6. Add 1/2 inch water to roasting pan and return roast to pan.
7. Cook at 300°F for about 3 Hours or until done.

Dr Pepper® Venison Roast

This is an interesting recipe.

Serves: 6

Preparation Time: 5 Minutes

Cooking Time: 8 Hours

Ingredients:
- 3 pound venison roast
- 1 can Dr Pepper®
- 2 cups water
- 1 tablespoon Worcestershire sauce
- ¼ teaspoon salt
- ¼ teaspoon pepper
- 3 cloves garlic

Preparation:
1. Place roast in crock pot. Add all other ingredients.
2. Cook for 8 Hours on low or until done. Drain off liquids and serve.

Mouthwatering, Easy Venison Roast

This recipe will make your roast melt in your mouth.

Serves: 6

Preparation Time: 5 Minutes

Cooking Time: 8 Hours

Ingredients:
- 3 to 5 pound venison roast
- 1 package brown gravy mix
- 1 package dried Italian salad dressing mix
- 1 package dried ranch salad dressing
- 1 cup water

Preparation:
1. Place roast in crock pot.
2. Mix dried ingredients together and sprinkle over roast.
3. Pour water around.
4. Cook for 8 Hours on low or until done.

Ginger Ale Venison Roast

A roast with a little different flavor.

Serves: 6

Preparation Time: 5 Minutes

Cooking Time: 8 Hours

Ingredients:
- 3 pound venison roast
- ½ cup flour
- 1 package dry onion soup mix
- 1 package brown gravy mix
- 2 cups ginger ale

Preparation:
1. Coat roast with flour. Place roast in crock pot.
2. Add mixture of soup mix, gravy mix, remaining flour and ginger ale.
3. Cook on low for 8 Hours or until tender.

Italian Venison Roast

This is a complete meal by itself.

Serves: 6

Preparation Time: 10 Minutes

Cooking Time: 8 Hours

Ingredients:
- 4 potatoes, peeled and quartered
- 2 cups baby carrots
- 1 celery stalk, cut in 2 inch lengths
- 1 small can diced tomatoes
- 3 pound venison roast
- 1 teaspoon black pepper
- 1 can condensed tomato soup
- ½ cup water
- 1 tablespoon garlic, chopped
- 1 teaspoon dried oregano leaves
- 1 teaspoon vinegar

Preparation:
1. Put potatoes, carrots, celery, and diced tomato in crock pot.
2. Sprinkle roast with black pepper. Place roast in crock pot.
3. Mix the soup, water, garlic, oregano and vinegar in a small bowl. Pour mixture over the roast.
4. Cook on low for 8 Hours or until done.

Tangy Marinated Venison Roast

This recipe will have people asking for seconds.

Serves: 6

Preparation Time: 10 Minutes (additional 12 Hours chill time)

Cooking Time: 8 Hours

Ingredients:
- ¼ cup green pepper, chopped
- ¼ cup onion, chopped
- ¼ cup celery, chopped
- ¼ cup vinegar
- 1½ teaspoon salt
- ½ teaspoon ground black pepper
- 3 tablespoons vegetable oil
- ¾ cup red wine
- 3 pound venison roast

Preparation:
1. Mix all ingredients except roast in a small bowl.
2. Place the roast in a large sealable plastic bag. Pour the marinade over the roast and seal.
3. Place in refrigerator for 12 Hours, turning occasionally.
4. Place roast and marinade in crock pot and cook for 8 Hours on low or until done.

Mexican Venison Roast

If you like Mexican food, this simple dish is something you'll love.

Serves: 6

Preparation Time: 10 Minutes

Cooking Time: 8 Hours

Ingredients:
- 3 pound venison roast
- 1½ cups beef broth
- 1 can diced tomatoes
- 1 can (4 ounces) chopped mild chile peppers
- 1 teaspoon ancho chile powder
- 1 teaspoon chili powder
- 1 teaspoon ground cumin
- 1 teaspoon onion powder
- ½ teaspoon garlic powder

Preparation:
1. Combine all ingredients in crock pot.
2. Cover and cook for 8 to 10 Hours on low or until done.

Nice & Easy Venison Roast

You can't find many dishes that are easier to prepare.

Serves: 6

Preparation Time: 10 Minutes

Cooking Time: 8 Hours

Ingredients:
- 3 pound venison roast
- 2 large carrots, chopped
- 1 onion, chopped
- 2 celery stalks, chopped
- 1 teaspoon garlic powder
- ½ teaspoon black pepper
- ½ cup Worcestershire sauce
- ½ cup barbeque sauce

Preparation:
1. Place roast in crock pot. Add carrots, onion, and celery.
2. Pour Worcestershire sauce and barbeque sauce over meat and vegetables.
3. Cook on low for 8 Hours or until done.

Pepsi® Venison Roast

A simple recipe with tasty results.

Serves: 6

Preparation Time: 5 Minutes

Cooking Time: 8 Hours

Ingredients:
- 3 pound venison roast
- 1 envelope dry onion soup mix
- 1 can cream of mushroom soup
- 12 ounces Pepsi®
- 2 large carrots, chopped
- 2 celery stalks, chopped

Preparation:
1. Place roast in crock pot.
2. Mix remaining ingredients and put in crock pot.
3. Cook on low for 8 Hours or until done.

Fantastic Crock Pot Venison Roast

Here's another crock pot recipe that everyone will enjoy.

Serves: 6

Preparation Time: 10 Minutes

Cooking Time: 8 Hours

Ingredients:
- 2 cans (10½ ounces) condensed cream of mushroom soup
- 1 envelope dry onion soup mix
- 1¼ cup water
- 3 pound venison roast

Preparation:
1. Mix cream of mushroom soup, dry onion soup mix and water in a bowl.
2. Place venison roast in crock pot.
3. Pour ingredients from bowl over the roast.
4. Cook on low for 8 Hours or until done.

Spicy Slow Cooker Venison Roast

This roast tastes as good as it smells.

Serves: 6

Preparation Time: 15 Minutes

Cooking Time: 5 Hours

Ingredients:
- 3 pound venison roast
- 4 garlic cloves, peeled
- 1 tablespoon chili powder
- ¼ teaspoon ground coriander
- ½ teaspoon ground cumin
- 2 cans (10½ ounces) condensed beef broth
- 2 cups onions, sliced
- 1 can whole peeled tomatoes
- 1 can red kidney beans, drained
- 1 cup uncooked regular long-grain rice

Preparation:
1. Cut 4 slits in the surface of the roast and stuff 1 clove garlic in each.
2. Stir the chili powder, coriander and cumin in a bowl. Rub the roast with the mixture.
3. Place the roast in the crock pot.
4. Stir the broth, onions, tomatoes, beans, and rice in a bowl. Pour the mixture over the roast.
5. Cook on High for 4 to 5 Hours or until done.

Spicy Oven Venison Roast

The additional 12 hour wait is worth the effort with this roast.

Serves: 6

Preparation Time: 5 Minutes (Additional 12 Hours Chill Time)

Cooking Time: 8 Hours

Ingredients:
- 3 tablespoons brown sugar
- 2 teaspoons ground cloves
- 2 teaspoons ground allspice
- 2 teaspoons ground cinnamon
- 1 teaspoon black pepper
- 3 pound venison roast
- 2 cups beef stock
- 1 bottle dark beer

Preparation:
1. Mix the brown sugar, cloves, allspice, and pepper in a large bowl.
2. Add the roast and turn to coat. Cover and refrigerate 12 Hours or overnight.
3. Preheat oven to 350°. Place the roast in 6-quart or greater baking pan.
4. Pour stock mixture and bottle of beer over roast. Cover with foil and bake for 3 Hours or until done.
5. Note if you prefer crock pot cooking: Place roast in a crock pot. Pour the stock and beer over the roast. Cook for 8 Hours on low or until done.

Tony's Venison Roast

This roast has been one of my favorites for years.

Serves: 6

Preparation Time: 15 Minute (Optional Overnight Soaking)

Cooking Time: 8 Hours

Ingredients:
- 3 pound venison roast
- 1 pound baby carrots
- 8–10 small potatoes, peeled
- 1 cup celery, chopped
- 1 onion, chopped
- 2-3 teaspoons Tony Chachere's® Creole Seasoning
- 2 cups water

Preparation:
(Optional) Soak the venison roast the day before in water with 3 teaspoons vinegar and then in regular water the night before.
1. Place the vegetables in the bottom of the crock pot.
2. Place the venison roast on top of the vegetables.
3. Add water to crock pot.
4. Sprinkle roast with creole seasoning.
5. Cook on low for 8 to 10 Hours or until done.

Veggie Venison Roast

Here's another way to make a venison roast that's delicious.

Serves: 6

Preparation Time: 15 Minutes

Cooking Time: 8 Hours

Ingredients:
- 6 slices bacon, halved crosswise
- 2 pounds red skinned potatoes, cut into chunks
- 8 carrots, peeled cut into 2 inch lengths and halved lengthwise
- Salt, to taste
- Pepper, to taste
- 1 teaspoon dried leaf thyme, divided
- 3 pound venison roast
- 1 bag frozen small onions
- 8 ounces mushrooms
- 1½ cup beef broth
- 3 tablespoons tomato paste
- 4 tablespoons water

Preparation:
1. Place bacon over the bottom of the crock pot. Arrange the carrots and potatoes over the bacon. Sprinkle lightly with salt, pepper, and half the thyme.
2. Place the roast in the crock pot on the veggies and then add the onions and mushrooms over and around the roast. Sprinkle lightly with salt , pepper and remaining thyme.
3. Mix the beef broth and tomato paste in a small bowl. Pour mixture over the roast.
4. Cook on low for 8 Hours or until done.

Venison Roast with Garlic Crust

This roast has an amazing flavor.

Serves: 6

Preparation Time: 15 Minutes

Cooking Time: 7 to 8 Hours

Ingredients:
- ¼ cup olive oil
- 3 cloves garlic, peeled and crushed
- 1 cup dry bread crumbs
- ¼ cup parsley, chopped
- 1 teaspoon salt
- 1 teaspoon black pepper
- 3 pound venison roast
- 1 cup water

Preparation:
1. Heat oil in skillet. Add garlic. Sauté 2 minutes pressing juice from garlic into oil. Discard garlic.
2. Mix in medium bowl bread crumbs, parsley, salt, and pepper.
3. Coat roast with garlic infused oil. Then press dry mixture onto roast, coating well.
4. Place roast in crock pot.
5. Add water and cook on low for 7 to 8 Hours or until done.

Venison Roast with Tomatoes

This crock pot roast turns out perfect every time.

Serves: 6

Preparation Time: 20 Minutes

Cooking Time: 8 Hours

Ingredients:
- 3 pound venison roast
- 2 tablespoons seasoned salt
- 1 tablespoon olive oil
- 1 onion, sliced
- 8 ounces mushrooms, sliced
- 1 can (10½ ounces) condensed French onion soup
- 1 teaspoon Worcestershire sauce
- 2 teaspoons ketchup
- 1 can diced tomatoes

Preparation:
1. Rub the roast all over with seasoned salt.
2. Heat olive oil in a large skillet over medium heat. Brown the roast on all sides.
3. Place roast in crock pot.
4. Sauté the onions and mushrooms in the skillet.
5. Add the soup, Worcestershire sauce, ketchup, and diced tomatoes and bring to a boil.
6. Pour over the roast in the crock pot.
7. Cook on high for 1 Hour.
8. Turn on low and continue cooking for 7 Hours or until done.

Chapter 2

Burgers

Zippy Burger

You can't have too many ways to prepare venison burgers.

Serves: 8

Prep Time: 25 Minutes

Cooking Time: Until desired doneness

Ingredients:
- ⅓ cup mayonnaise
- 1 teaspoon lime juice
- 2 tablespoons Dijon mustard
- ½ teaspoon grated lime peel
- ⅓ cup onion, chopped
- 3 tablespoons plain yogurt
- 2 tablespoons chopped jalapeno peppers
- 1 teaspoon salt
- 1 teaspoon pepper
- 2 pounds ground venison
- 8 slices pepper jack cheese

Preparation:
1. Combine the mayonnaise, lime juice, mustard and lime peel in a bowl. Cover and refrigerate.
2. In a large bowl mix the onions, yogurt, jalapeno, salt, pepper, and venison. When well blended shape into 8 patties and fry or grill till desired doneness.
3. Top with mayo mix and cheese slices and serve.

Venison Beer Burgers

These burgers are great using the ground venison in your freezer.

Serves: 6

Preparation Time: 10 Minutes (Note: Needs overnight refrigeration)

Cooking Time: Till desired doneness

Ingredients:
- 2 pounds ground venison
- Salt
- Pepper
- 2- 12 ounce cans beer

Preparation Time:
1. Season the meat to taste with salt and pepper.
2. Shape into 6 patties and place in a glass baking dish.
3. Pour the beer over the patties, cover and refrigerate overnight.
4. Remove the patties from the beer and fry or grill to your satisfaction.

Tasty Venison Burgers

This is just another great way to enjoy venison.

Serves: 4

Preparation Time: 10 Minutes

Cooking Time: To meet individual preference.

Ingredients:
- 1 pound ground venison
- ½ cup rolled oats
- ¼ cup ketchup
- ½ cup onion, chopped
- 1 egg, lightly beaten
- 2 teaspoons Dijon mustard
- 2 cloves garlic, minced
- 1 teaspoon salt
- 1 teaspoon Worcestershire sauce
- 1 teaspoon black pepper

Preparation:
1. Combine all ingredients in a large bowl.
2. Shape into patties and fry or grill to meet personal preferences.

Special Venison Burgers

These burgers are tasty with a little bit of a bite.

Serves: 4

Preparation Time: 10 Minutes

Cooking Time: Till desired doneness

Ingredients:
- 1 pound ground venison
- 1½ teaspoons horseradish
- 1 onion, chopped
- ¼ cup evaporated milk
- 1 teaspoon salt
- ½ teaspoon pepper
- 2 teaspoons prepared mustard
- 3 tablespoons ketchup
- ½ cup dried bread crumbs

Preparation:
1. Combine all ingredients in a large bowl until well blended. Shape into 4 patties.
2. Fry or grill patties to your satisfaction.

Smoke Tasting Burgers

This recipe gives your burgers a little different taste.

Serves: 8

Preparation Time: 10 Minutes

Cooking Time: Till desired doneness

Ingredients:
- 1 pound ground venison
- 1 pound ground beef
- ¼ cup bread crumbs
- 1 egg, slightly beaten
- ¼ cup onion, chopped
- 2 tablespoons green pepper, chopped
- 1 teaspoon salt
- 1 teaspoon black pepper
- 1 teaspoon paprika
- 2 teaspoons liquid smoke
- ½ teaspoon cayenne pepper

Preparation:
1. Combine all ingredients and mix until well blended.
2. Shape into 8 patties and grill or fry to meet individual preference.

Camp Venison Burgers

A simple recipe that you'll like the first time you try it.

Serves: 4

Preparation Time: 10 Minutes

Cooking Time: To individual required doneness.

Ingredients:
- 1 pound ground venison
- 3 tablespoons evaporated milk
- 1 teaspoon garlic salt
- Salt, to taste
- Pepper, to taste
- 1 egg, slightly beaten
- 1 teaspoon onion salt
- 1 teaspoon prepared mustard

Preparation:
1. Combine all ingredients until well blended. Shape mixture into 4 patties.
2. Fry or grill to individual tastes.

Bambi Venison Burger

This is just another one of my favorite simple recipes.

Serves: 4

Preparation Time: 10 Minutes

Cooking Time: Till desired doneness

Ingredients:
- 1 pound ground venison
- 2 teaspoons horseradish
- 1½ teaspoons Worcestershire sauce
- 1 onion, chopped
- ¼ cup evaporated milk
- 1 teaspoon salt
- 2 teaspoons prepared mustard
- 4 tablespoons ketchup
- ½ cup bread crumbs

Preparation:
1. Combine all ingredients and mix until well blended. Shape into patties.
2. Fry or grill patties until done to your satisfaction.

Barbeque Venison Burgers

The flavor of these burgers will appeal to a lot of people.

Serves: 6

Preparation Time: 10 Minutes

Cooking Time: 50 Minutes

Ingredients:
- 1 pound ground venison
- ½ pound ground pork
- 1 tablespoon garlic powder
- 1 teaspoon salt
- 1 teaspoon pepper
- 1 teaspoon accent
- ½ cup water
- 1 (16 ounce) bottle barbeque sauce

Preparation:
1. Mix all ingredients except water and barbeque sauce.
2. When well blended shape into 6 patties.
3. Brown mixture in a large skillet.
4. Drain grease and add the water and barbeque sauce.
5. Cover and let simmer for 45 Minutes.

Burgers with a Jalapeno Kick

If you enjoy hot stuff, this might become your favorite way to prepare burgers.

Serves: 4

Preparation Time: 10 Minutes

Cooking Time: Till desired doneness.

Ingredients:
- 1 pound ground venison
- ¼ cup jalapeno peppers, seeded and chopped
- 1 egg, slightly beaten
- ¼ cup bread crumbs
- 4 slices Monterey Jack cheese

Preparation:
1. Combine all the ingredients except the cheese until well blended.
2. Shape mixture into 4 patties.
3. Grill or fry patties to desired doneness.
4. Top each burger with a cheese slice until the cheese is melted.

Mandy's Jr. Venison Bacon Burgers

Everything seems to taste just a bit better with bacon.

Serves: 6

Preparation Time: 35 Minutes

Cooking Time: Till desired doneness.

Ingredients:
- 6 slices bacon (minced)
- 2 tablespoons olive oil
- 1 teaspoon garlic, minced
- 2 shallot, minced
- 2 pounds ground venison
- 2 tablespoons Worcestershire sauce
- 1 tablespoon fresh parsley, chopped
- ¼ teaspoon salt
- ½ teaspoon pepper
- 1 egg, lightly beaten

Preparation:
1. Cook bacon in a skillet until crispy. Pour bacon and grease into a metal bowl and let cool.
2. Heat olive oil in skillet, add garlic and shallots, stir and cook until softened. Add bacon and let cool.
3. Mix in the venison, Worcestershire sauce, parsley, salt, pepper, and egg. Stir until evenly blended.
4. Refrigerate for 30 Minutes.
5. Shape into 6 patties and fry or grill to meet personal preferences.

Hawaiian Venison Burgers

This unusual recipe has been in my collection for years.

Serves: 6

Preparation Time: 15 Minutes

Cooking Time: 15-20 Minutes

Ingredients:
- 1½ pounds ground venison
- 1 can (8 ounces) pineapple slices in juice, undrained
- 1 can (10½ ounce) condensed French onion soup
- 2 teaspoons brown sugar
- 1 tablespoon apple cider vinegar

Preparation:
1. Shape the venison into 6 burgers (approximately ½ inch thick).
2. Stir the soup, pineapple juice (reserve the pineapple slices separately), sugar and vinegar into a small bowl and put to the side.
3. Cook burgers in skillet over medium-high heat until well browned on both sides. Pour off any fat. Top each burger with one slice of pineapple.
4. Add the soup mixture to the skillet and heat to a boil. Reduce heat to low. Cover and cook for 5 Minutes or until the burger are cooked.

Melt In Your Mouth Onion Burgers

You can't help but love the ease of preparation with this recipe.

Serves: 6

Preparation Time: 5 Minutes

Cooking Time: 10 Minutes or to your desired doneness

Ingredients:
- 1½ pounds ground venison
- 1 envelope (1 ounce) dry onion soup and recipe mix
- 3 tablespoons water

Preparation:
- Thoroughly mix the venison, soup mix and water. Shape into 6 burgers (approximately ½ inch thick).
- Cook the burgers over medium-high heat until brown on both sides (approximately 10 Minutes for medium or to your desired doneness).

Chapter 3

Meatloafs

Simple Meatloaf

This may become the recipe that you'll be making the most.

Serves: 6

Preparation: 10 Minutes

Cooking Time: 1 Hour 10 Minutes

Ingredients:
- 2 pounds ground venison
- 2 eggs, lightly beaten
- ½ cup milk
- 1 cup plain bread crumbs
- 2 tablespoons dried minced onion
- 1½ teaspoons burger seasoning
- ½ cup ketchup

Preparation:
1. Heat oven to 350°F.
2. Mix all ingredients until well blended and shape into a greased 9 x 5 inch loaf pan.
3. Bake for 1 Hour and 10 Minutes. Let cool and serve.

Toni's Italian Meatloaf

This is a recipe that will surprise you with its fantastic flavor.

Serves: 8

Preparation Time: 15 Minutes

Cooking Time: 1 Hour 20 Minutes

Ingredients:
- 2 pounds ground venison
- 1 cup spaghetti sauce, divided into two
- 1½ cups herb seasoned stuffing
- 1 cup onion, chopped
- 2 eggs, lightly beaten
- ½ cup shredded mozzarella cheese

Preparation:
1. Preheat oven to 350°F.
2. Mix the venison, ½ cup sauce, onion, stuffing and eggs in a large bowl until well blended.
3. Pack firmly into a greased 9 x 5 inch loaf pan.
4. Bake at for 1 Hour 15 Minutes or until thoroughly cooked.
5. Spoon the remaining sauce over the loaf and sprinkle with the cheese.
6. Bake an additional 5 Minutes or until the cheese is melted.

Meatloaf with Onion Crunch Topping

A great recipe to prepare a delicious meatloaf.

Serves: 6

Prep Time: 10 Minutes

Cooking Time: 1 Hour

Ingredients:
- 1 can tomato soup, divided in two
- 1½ pounds ground venison
- 1 egg, lightly beaten
- 1 can French Fried Onions (28 ounces), divided
- 1 tablespoon Worcestershire sauce

Preparation:
1. Preheat oven to 400°F.
2. Mix ½ can tomato soup, venison, egg, ½ of the can of onions, and Worcestershire sauce in a large bowl until well blended.
3. Firmly place mixture in a greased 9 x 5 inch loaf pan.
4. Spoon the remaining soup over the loaf. Bake at 400°F for 1 Hour or until done.
5. Sprinkle the remaining onions over the top and bake for 3 Minutes. Serve hot.

Jonny Applesauce Meatloaf

You are certain to get compliments on this meatloaf.

Serves: 6

Prep Time: 10 Minutes

Cooking Time: 1 Hour 45 Minutes

Ingredients:
- 2 pounds ground venison
- ½ cup onion, chopped
- 1 egg, lightly beaten
- ¾ cup applesauce
- 1 cup dry bread crumbs
- 2½ tablespoons ketchup
- 2 teaspoons salt
- ¼ teaspoon black pepper

Preparation:
1. Preheat oven to 350°F.
2. Mix all ingredients in a large bowl until well blended.
3. Place the mixture into a greased 9 x 5 inch loaf pan.
4. Bake for 1 Hour and 30 Minutes or until done. Let stand 10 minutes before slicing.

Cheesy Meatloaf

A little bit different meatloaf with a cheesy flavor.

Serves: 8

Prep Time: 15 Minutes

Cooking Time: 1 Hour

Ingredients:
- 2 pounds ground venison
- 1½ cups shredded cheddar cheese
- ¼ cup milk
- ½ cup plain dry bread crumbs
- ¼ cup chunky salsa
- 1 egg, lightly beaten
- 1 clove garlic, minced

Preparation:
1. Preheat oven to 400°F.
2. Mix all ingredients until well blended.
3. Shape into loaf in a greased 9 x 5 inch loaf pan.
4. Bake 1 Hour or until center is no longer pink.
5. Let sit 10 Minutes and cut into 8 slices.

Worcestershire Venison Meatloaf

This meatloaf has an amazing flavor.

Serves: 8

Prep Time: 10 Minutes

Cooking Time: 1 Hour 15 Minutes

Ingredients:
- 2 pounds ground venison
- ¾ cup tomato juice
- ½ cup dry bread crumbs
- 1 slightly beaten egg
- ½ cup onion, chopped
- 2 tablespoons prepared horseradish
- 1 tablespoon Worcestershire sauce
- ¼ teaspoon ground black pepper
- 2 slices processed American cheese

Preparation:
1. Preheat over to 350°F.
2. Thoroughly mix all ingredients except the cheese slices in a large bowl until well blended.
3. Pack the mixture into a greased   9 x 5 inch loaf pan and bake for 1 Hour and 10 Minutes.
4. Place the cheese on the meatloaf for 5 Minutes or until the meatloaf is cooked. Let stand 10 Minutes before slicing.

Black Bean & Venison Meatloaf

A different meatloaf with a southern flair.

Serves: 6

Preparation: 20 Minutes

Cooking Time: 1 Hour 15 Minutes

Ingredients:
- 2 pounds ground venison
- 1 can (15 ounce) black beans, drained and rinsed
- ½ teaspoon garlic powder
- ¾ teaspoon ground cumin
- ¼ cup onion, chopped
- 1 tablespoon chili powder
- ½ teaspoon salt
- ¼ teaspoon ground black pepper
- 1 egg, lightly beaten
- ⅓ cup dry bread crumbs
- ¼ cup milk
- 1 cup shredded Mexican cheeses
- Salsa (optional)

Preparation:
1. Preheat over to 350⁰F.
2. Combine all the ingredients in a large bowl and mix until well blended.
3. Pack in a greased 9 x 5 inch loaf pan and bake for 1 Hour 15 Minutes.
4. If desired, spoon a little salsa over the loaf and continue to bake for 5 additional Minutes.

George's Best Meatloaf

The name of this recipe tells you this is one of my favorite ways to make meatloaf.

Serves: 6

Prep Time: 10 Minutes

Cooking Time: 1 Hour 15 Minutes

Ingredients:
- 2 pounds ground venison
- ½ cup tomato soup
- 1 envelope dry onion soup mix
- ½ cup plain dry bread crumbs
- 1 egg, lightly beaten

Preparation:
1. Preheat oven to 350°F.
2. Mix all ingredients in a large bowl until well blended.
3. Shape mixture into a greased 9 x 5 inch loaf pan and bake at for 1 Hour and 15 Minutes. Let stand at least 10 Minutes before slicing.

My Stuffed Meatloaf

This unique preparation will provide a meal to remember.

Serves: 8

Prep Time: 20 Minutes

Cooking Time: 45 Minutes

Ingredients:
- 2 pounds ground venison
- 2 eggs, lightly beaten and divided
- ¼ cup steak sauce (such as A1 Original Steak Sauce®)
- ½ yellow onion, chopped and divided
- 1 teaspoon salt
- ¼ teaspoon black pepper
- 1 cup crushed buttery crackers (about 25) (such as Ritz Crackers®)
- ½ cup celery, chopped
- ¼ cup walnut pieces
- 1 teaspoon poultry seasoning

Preparation:
1. Preheat oven to 350°F and lightly grease a 13 x 9 inch dish.
2. Mix venison, 1 egg, steak sauce, half the onion, salt and pepper in a large bowl until well blended.
3. Press mixture into a 12 x 10 inch rectangle pan on wax paper.
4. In separate bowl - mix crackers, celery, walnut pieces, poultry seasoning, remaining egg and remaining onion until well blended.
5. Spread mixture over meat mixture to within 1 inch of edges and press lightly into meat mixture.
6. Roll up from one of the short ends as for a jelly roll, removing the wax paper as it is rolled. Press ends and edges together to seal.
7. Place in a 13 x 9 inch dish and bake for 45 Minutes or until done.

Number One Meatloaf

This recipe features ease of preparation with great results.

Serves: 8

Prep Time: 10 Minutes

Cooking Time: 1 Hour

Ingredients:
- 1 can tomato sauce (8 ounces), divided in two
- 2 pounds ground venison
- 1 onion, chopped
- ⅓ cup steak sauce (such as A1 Original Steak Sauce®)
- 1 cup dry bread crumbs
- 2 eggs, lightly beaten
- ½ teaspoon ground black pepper

Preparation:
1. Preheat oven to 350°F and lightly grease a 9 x 5 inch loaf pan.
2. Thoroughly mix all ingredients except the other divided half of the tomato sauce in a large bowl until well blended. Shape meat mixture into the loaf pan.
3. Bake for 50 Minutes. Remove and drain fat from pan and top meatloaf with remaining tomato sauce and bake for an additional 10 Minutes or until done. Let stand 5 Minutes before slicing.

Onion Meatloaf

This is just another great way to prepare a venison meatloaf.

Serves: 6

Preparation: 20 Minutes

Cooking Time: 1 Hour 25 Minutes

Ingredients:
For Loaf:
- 2 cups onion, diced
- 2 tablespoons butter
- 1 tablespoon balsamic vinegar
- 2 pounds ground venison
- 1 teaspoon salt
- ¼ teaspoon ground savory

For Topping:
- ½ cup ketchup
- ¼ cup brown sugar
- 2 tablespoons balsamic vinegar
- 1 teaspoon mustard

Preparation:
1. Preheat oven to 350^{0}F and grease a 9 x 5 inch loaf pan.
2. Sauté the onion in butter in a saucepan for about 7 Minutes. Add balsamic vinegar and sauté an additional Minute.
3. Combine all of the other loaf ingredients until well blended and stir in onion mixture.
4. Shape meat into loaf pan and bake for 1 Hour and 15 Minutes.
5. While meatloaf is baking, bring topping ingredients to a boil in a saucepan, stirring mixture.
6. Remove meatloaf from oven and spoon topping over the loaf and bake about 12 Minutes. Let stand for 10 Minutes before slicing.

Mushroom Meatloaf

Good summertime meal when the veggies are fresh.

Serves: 4

Preparation Time: 10 Minutes

Cooking Time: 1 Hour 15 Minutes

Ingredients:
- 1 pound ground venison
- 1 small summer squash, finely chopped
- 1 small onion, finely chopped
- 6 ounces mushrooms, minced
- 1 egg, lightly beaten
- ½ cup dry bread crumbs
- Dash garlic powder
- ¾ teaspoon salt
- ⅛ teaspoon ground black pepper

Preparation:
1. Preheat oven to 350°F.
2. Mix all ingredients in a large bowl until well blended. Shape into loaf and place in a greased 9 x 5 inch loaf pan.
3. Bake for 1 Hour and 15 Minutes.

Pepper Meatloaf

This recipe is a good way to use up some of those peppers you've been growing.

Serves: 8

Preparation Time: 10 Minutes

Cooking Time: 1 Hour 15 Minutes

Ingredients:
- 2 pounds ground venison
- ½ cup dry bread crumbs
- ½ cup chili sauce
- ¼ cup beef broth
- 1 egg, lightly beaten
- 1 green bell pepper, coarsely chopped
- 1 red bell pepper, coarsely chopped
- 1 orange bell pepper, coarsely chopped
- 1 onion, coarsely chopped
- 1 teaspoon salt
- ½ teaspoon ground black pepper
- Dash Cajun seasoning

Preparation:
1. Preheat oven to 350°F.
2. Mix all ingredients in a large bowl until well blended.
3. Pack into a greased 9 x 5 inch loaf pan and bake 1 Hour and 15 Minutes.

Salsa Tortilla Meatloaf

Try this simple recipe. I know you'll like it.

Serves: 8

Preparation Time: 10 Minutes

Cooking Time: 1 Hour

Ingredients:
- 1½ pounds ground venison
- 1 egg, lightly beaten
- 1⅓ cups Salsa, divided into two
- ¾ cup tortilla chips, finely crushed
- ½ cup green onions, minced

Preparation:
1. Preheat over to 350°F.
2. Mix ingredients except the remaining ½ of salsa in a large bowl until well blended.
3. Pack the mixture into a greased 9x5 inch loaf pan.
4. Top with the remaining salsa.
5. Bake for 1 Hour or until cooked. Let stand 10 Minutes before slicing.

Matt's Barbecue Meatloaf

Barbeque sauce is the perfect way to spice up meatloaf.

Serves: 4

Preparation Time : 10 Minutes

Cooking Time: 45 Minutes

Ingredients:
- 1 pound ground venison
- ½ cup thick and spicy barbeque sauce, divided
- ½ cup old fashioned oats
- ½ cup onion, finely chopped
- 1 egg, lightly beaten

Preparation:
1. Preheat oven to 375°.
2. Mix all ingredients in a large bowl until well blended saving ¼ cup of the barbeque sauce.
3. Shape into a greased 9 x5 inch loaf pan or baking dish. Bake at 375° F for 45 Minutes.
4. Top with the saved ¼ cup barbeque sauce.

Mini-Cheddar Meatloaves

This recipe produces eight mini loaves. Eat two and freeze the rest.

Serves: 4

Preparation Time: 15 Minutes

Cooking Time : 45 Minutes

Ingredients:
- 1 egg
- ¾ cup milk
- 1 cup shredded Cheddar cheese
- ½ cup quick rolled oats
- ½ cup onion, chopped
- 1 teaspoon salt
- 1 pound ground venison
- ⅔ cup ketchup
- ½ cup brown sugar
- 1½ teaspoons yellow mustard

Preparation:
1. Preheat oven to 350° F.
2. Beat the egg and milk in a large bowl. Stir in the cheese, oats, onion and salt.
3. Add the venison and mix thoroughly. Shape the venison mixture into 8 loaves.
4. Place the loaves into a greased 13 x 9 x 2 inch baking pan.
5. Stir the ketchup, brown sugar and mustard in a small bowl and spoon the mixture over the loaves.
6. Bake for 45 Minutes at 350°F.

Chapter 4

Chili

Mighty Hot Chili

This chili is hot and tasty.

Serves: 6

Preparation Time: 10 Minutes

Cooking Time: 8 Hours

Ingredients:
- 1½ pounds ground venison
- 2 chopped onions
- 1 (15 ounce) can red kidney beans
- 1/2 chopped green pepper
- 3 cups water
- 2 (6 ounce) cans tomato paste
- 1 (15 ounce) can diced tomatoes
- 1 (4 ounce) can diced green chili peppers
- 6 cloves garlic, minced
- 1 tablespoon yellow mustard
- 1 teaspoon chili powder
- 1 teaspoon ground black pepper
- ½ teaspoon ground cumin
- ½ teaspoon salt
- 1 teaspoon cayenne pepper

Preparation:
1. Cook venison and onion in a large skillet until brown.
2. Put venison mixture in a crockpot.
3. Add all other ingredients and stir until well blended.
4. Cook on low for 8 Hours or until done.

Meaty Chili

A meatlovers dish that is certain to please.

Serves: 6

Preparation Time: 10 Minutes

Cooking Time: 1 Hour

Ingredients:
- 1 pound ground venison
- 2 (15 ounce) cans spicy Mexican-style beans
- 1 (15 ounce) can corn, drained
- 2 (15 ounce) can of chili without beans
- 1 (12 ounce) can of Span, drained and cubed
- 1 (15 ounce) can Vienna sausage, drained and sliced
- Quarter pound Colby cheese, cubed

Preparation:
1. Brown the venison in a large frying pan.
2. Add the beans, refried beans, corn, chili, Spam, and Vienna sausages.
3. Bring to a boil, stirring occasionally.
4. Mix in the Colby cheese and simmer for 1 Hour.

Uncle Mike's Crockpot Chili

Cook this all day in your crockpot and your meal will be ready when you get home.

Serves: 8

Preparation Time: 15 Minutes

Cooking Time: 9 Hours

Ingredients:
- 2 pounds ground venison
- 1 large can tomato juice
- 2 (15 ounce) cans tomato sauce
- 1 (15 ounce) can red kidney beans, drained
- 1 (15 ounce) can pinto beans, drained
- 2 cups chopped onions
- ¼ cup chopped green pepper
- ⅛ teaspoon ground cayenne pepper
- 1 teaspoon sugar
- 1 teaspoon dried oregano
- 1 teaspoon ground black pepper
- 1 teaspoon salt
- 2 teaspoons ground cumin
- ¼ cup chili powder

Preparation:
1. Brown venison in a large skillet.
2. Add all the other ingredients and mix well.
3. Bring to a boil, reduce heat and simmer for 1 Hour.
4. Transfer everything into a crockpot and cook on low for 8 Hours or until done.

Quick Chili with Beans

Another chili recipe that you can be certain will result in a great meal.

Serves: 6

Preparation Time: 15 Minutes

Cooking Time: 2 Hours

Ingredients:
- 2 pounds ground venison
- 1 chopped onion
- 2 minced garlic cloves
- 1 (15 ounce) can tomato sauce
- 1 (6 ounce) can tomato paste
- 1 (15 ounce) can diced tomatoes with green chilies
- 1 (12 ounce) can beer
- 1 tablespoon ground cumin
- 1 teaspoon paprika
- 2 teaspoons chili powder
- 1 teaspoon oregano
- 1 teaspoon salt
- 1 teaspoon pepper
- 1 teaspoon Worcestershire sauce
- 1 (28 ounce) can chili beans

Preparation:
1. Sauté the venison, onions and garlic in a large skillet.
2. Add the remaining ingredients, stir well, cover and simmer for 2 Hours.

Easiest Chili Yet

This chili is as delicious as it is easy to prepare.

Serves: 6

Preparation Time: 10 Minutes

Cooking Time: 8 Hours

Ingredients:
- 1 pound ground venison
- ½ chopped onion
- ½ chopped green pepper
- 1 (15 ounce) can tomato sauce
- 1 (10 ounce) can chili beans
- 1 (10 ounce) can tomato soup
- 2 tablespoons chili powder

Preparation:
1. Brown venison in a skillet.
2. Put browned venison in a crockpot , add all other ingredients and stir well.
3. Cook on low for 8 Hours or until done.

Taco Chili in a Crockpot

A simple chili with a Mexican flavor.

Serves: 6 - 8

Preparation Time: 15 Minutes

Cooking Time: 8 Hours

Ingredients:
- 1½ pound ground venison
- 1 chopped onion
- 2 ounces taco seasoning
- 28 ounces diced tomatoes
- 10 ounces diced tomatoes with green chilies
- 16 ounces rinsed and drained pinto beans
- 15 ounces pinto beans in chili sauce
- 1 cup whole kernel corn
- Shredded cheddar cheese
- Slightly crushed tortilla chips

Preparation:
1. Place venison in a skillet and add onions . Cook until meat is brown and onions tender.
2. Put mixture into a crockpot.
3. Stir in dry taco seasoning, diced tomatoes, diced tomatoes with green chiles, pinto beans, chili beans in chili sauce, and corn.
4. Cook on low for 8 Hours or until done.
5. Sprinkle each serving with some cheese and crushed chips.

Venison and Black Bean Chili

This recipe comes from one of my Southern relatives.

Serves: 8

Preparation Time: 10 Minutes

Cooking Time: 1Hour 10 Minutes

Ingredients:
- 3 teaspoons olive oil, divided
- 1½ pound ground venison
- 1 teaspoon salt
- 1 chopped onion
- 3 cloves garlic, minced
- 1 tablespoon chile powder
- 1 tablespoon ground cumin
- 1 teaspoon dried oregano
- 1 teaspoon ground cinnamon
- 1½ cups chicken broth
- 1 cup water
- 1 (28 ounce) can crushed fire-roasted tomatoes
- 2 tablespoons tomato paste
- 2 tablespoons honey
- 1 (15 ounce) can black beans, rinsed and drained
- 1 tablespoon fresh lime juice

Preparation:
1. Heat 1 teaspoon oil in a heavy Dutch oven over medium heat. Add venison and brown.
2. Transfer venison to a small bowl, sprinkle with salt and set aside. Add the remaining 2 teaspoons oil to the Dutch oven.
3. Add onion and sauté till soft but not browned. Add garlic and sauté about another minute.
4. Stir in the chili powder, cumin, oregano, and cinnamon. Cook another minute.
5. Add chicken broth, water, browned venison, crushed tomatoes, tomato paste and honey.
6. Reduce heat to medium-low and simmer for 1 Hour, stirring occasionally.
7. Add beans and lime juice and cook for an additional 5 Minutes.

Venison Recipes Made Simple

Nuclear Chili

You might want to have a cold drink handy with this dish.

Serves: 8

Preparation Time: 30 Minutes

Cooking Time: 5 Hours

Ingredients:
- 2 pounds ground venison
- 1 chopped onion
- 1 tablespoon crushed red pepper
- 3 tablespoons garlic powder
- 1 tablespoon seasoned pepper
- 1 (8 ounce) can mushroom pieces
- 1 (28 ounce) can baked beans
- 2 (15 ounce) cans red kidney beans
- 2 (6 ounce) cans tomato paste
- ¼ cup white sugar
- 4 sliced carrots
- 3 sliced celery stalks
- 1 chopped green bell pepper
- 1 chopped red bell pepper
- 2 chopped jalapeno chile peppers
- ½ cup beer
- 3 tablespoons hot sauce
- ¼ cup barbeque sauce

Preparation:
1. In a large skillet over medium heat, brown ground venison with onion, red pepper, garlic powder ,and seasoned pepper. Place mixture into a crackpot.
2. Stir mushrooms, baked beans, kidney beans, tomato paste, sugar, carrots, celery, peppers, beer, and barbeque sauce into the crockpot.
3. Add the hot sauce and more red pepper.
4. Cook on low for 5 Hours or until done.

My Sister's Chili

This chili recipe comes from my Sister and is a dish I've fed to non-hunters that they love.

Serves: 6

Preparation Time: 10 Minutes

Cooking Time: 8 Hours

Ingredients:
- 1 chopped onion
- 1 chopped green pepper
- 1½ pounds ground venison
- 1 large can diced tomatoes
- 1 small can tomato sauce
- 1 can red kidney beans
- 1 can chili beans
- 2 tablespoons sugar
- Salt, to taste

Preparation:
1. In a large skillet over medium heat, brown the ground venison together with the onion and pepper.
2. Stir in the other ingredients, cover and simmer for 1 Hour.
3. Transfer contents to a crockpot and cook on low for 7 Hours.

Winning Venison Chili

This crockpot creation should be a blue ribbon winner.

Serves: 8

Preparation Time: 15 Minutes

Cooking Time: 8 Hours

Ingredients:
- 3 pounds ground venison
- 4 tablespoons butter
- 3 tablespoons cooking oil
- 3 (15 oz) cans red kidney beans
- 1½ cups tomato sauce
- ¾ cup of tomato paste
- 1 can diced tomato
- 6 cloves garlic, chopped
- 6 Jalapeno peppers, chopped
- 1 green bell pepper, chopped
- 1 onion, chopped
- ½ cup barbeque sauce
- ½ cup water
- 2 tablespoons redhot sauce
- 3 tablespoons Worchestershire sauce
- 3 tablespoons chili powder
- 2 tablespoons honey
- 1 tablespoon oregano
- 1 teaspoon cayenne pepper
- 1 teaspoon salt

Preparation:
1. Brown the venison in a large skillet in the butter and oil.
2. Add the onion and garlic to the browned venison and cook until softened.
3. Place the browned venison mix in a crockpot and add the remaining ingredients stirring well.
4. Cook on high for 2 Hours and then on low for another 6 Hours or until done.

Chapter 5

Meatballs, Pasta & More

Hot Italian Venison Meatballs

These meatballs will spice up your spaghetti dinner.

Serves: 4

Preparation Time: 10 Minutes

Cooking Time: 20 Minutes

Ingredients:
- 1 pound ground venison
- 2 eggs, slightly beaten
- 1 cup Italian bread crumbs
- ¼ cup grated Parmesian cheese
- 3 cloves garlic, minced
- 1 tablespoon ground oregano
- 1 teaspoon caraway seeds
- 1 tablespoon cayenne pepper
- ⅛ teaspoon black pepper

Preparation:
1. Preheat the oven to 375°F.
2. Mix all the ingredients in a large bowl until well blended.
3. Shape mixture into golf size meatballs.
4. Place meatballs on an ungreased cookie sheet.
5. Bake for 10 minutes and flip.
6. Bake for an additional 10 minutes or until done.

Little Venison Meatballs

A great addition to your next party.

Serves: 60 Appetizers

Preparation Time: 15 Minutes

Cooking Time: 45 Minutes

Ingredients:
- 1 pound ground venison
- ½ cup dry bread crumbs
- ½ cup onions, finely chopped
- ¼ cup evaporated milk
- 1 egg, slightly beaten
- 1 tablespoon parsley
- 1 teaspoon pepper
- ¼ teaspoon salt
- ½ teaspoon Worcestershire sauce
- ¼ cup shortening
- 12 ounces chili sauce
- 10 ounces grape jelly

Preparation:
1. In a large bowl mix all the ingredients except the shortening, chili sauce and grape jelly.
2. When well blended, shape mixture into 1-inch meatballs.
3. Add shortening to a large skillet and brown meatballs.
4. Remove meatballs from skillet and drain grease.
5. Heat chili and jelly in skillet stirring until melted.
6. Add meatballs and stir until thoroughly cooked.
7. Simmer uncovered for 30 Minutes.

One Skillet Venison Italian Pasta

People don't realize they are eating venison with this dish.

Serves: 8

Preparation Time: 10 Minutes

Cooking Time: 20 Minutes

Ingredients:
- 2 pounds ground venison
- 2 cloves garlic, minced
- 1 can diced tomatoes
- 1 can beef broth
- 1 cup water
- 2 cups bow tie pasta, uncooked
- 2 zucchini, sliced
- 1 small can tomato paste
- ½ teaspoon Italian seasoning
- 1 cup shredded Cheddar cheese

Preparation:
1. Brown the venison and garlic in a large skillet. Drain off any grease.
2. Add the diced tomatoes, the broth and the water.
3. Mix well and bring to a boil.
4. Add the pasta and zucchini mix well and cover.
5. Reduce heat to medium and simmer for 15 Minutes.
6. Stir in the tomato paste and Italian seasoning until well blended.
7. Sprinkle with cheese and serve.

Party Time Venison Meatballs

Your guest will be smacking their lips for more after eating this appetizer.

Serves: 60

Preparation Time: 20 Minutes

Cooking Time: 20 Minutes

Ingredients:
- 1½ pounds ground venison
- ⅓ cup onion, chopped
- ⅓ cup dry bread crumbs
- 1 egg, lightly beaten
- ⅛ teaspoon black pepper
- 1 can condensed mushroom soup
- ½ cup sour cream
- ¼ cup water
- 2 teaspoons Worcestershire sauce
- Chopped fresh parsley

Preparation:
1. Mix the venison, onion, bread crumbs, egg and pepper in a large bowl until well blended.
2. Shape the mixture into 60 (1-inch) meatballs.
3. Place the meatballs in a 15 x 10 baking pan.
4. Broil the meatball for 5 Minutes or until browned, turning the meatballs over halfway through cooking.
5. In a large skillet add the soup, sour cream and Worcestershire sauce and stir.
6. Add the meatballs and cook over low heat for 10 Minutes or until done, stirring occasionally.
7. Sprinkle with parsley.

Pittsburgh Venison Meatballs

These are just a great addition to your next pasta meal.

Serves: 6

Preparation Time: 10 Minutes

Cooking Time: 10 Minutes

Ingredients:
- 1 pound ground venison
- ⅔ cup bread crumbs
- 1 onion, finely chopped
- 2 teaspoons dried parsley
- 1 teaspoon garlic powder
- ⅓ cup milk
- 2 eggs, lightly beaten
- Salt and pepper to taste

Preparation:
1. Add all the ingredients except the venison in a large bowl and mix.
2. Add the venison and mix until well blended.
3. Shape into ¾ inch meatballs.
4. Cook in a large non-stick frying pan on medium heat for 10 Minutes (or until browned) stirring occasionally.
5. Remove and drain on a paper towel.

Skillet Picante Venison Stroganoff

This is one of those dishes that never fails to please.

Serves: 4

Preparation Time: 20 Minutes

Cooking Time: 20 Minutes

Ingredients:
- 1 pound ground venison
- 3 cups sliced mushrooms
- 1 (16 ounce) jar picante sauce
- ⅓ cup sour cream
- 4 cups medium egg noodle, cooked and drained
- 1 tablespoon fresh parsley, chopped

Preparation:
1. Place the venison in a skillet over medium heat and stir until well browned. Drain any grease.
2. Add the mushrooms, stir and cook until the mushrooms are tender.
3. Stir in the picante sauce and bring to a boil. Stir in the sour cream.
4. Serve the mixture over the noodle. Sprinkle with the parsley.

The Swede's Venison Meatballs

It's hard to find someone who doesn't like these meatballs over noodles.

Serves: 6

Cooking Time: 10 Minutes

Preparation Time: 20 Minutes

Ingredients:
- 1 lightly beaten egg
- 1pound ground venison
- 1 cup stove top stuffing
- ½ cup milk
- ½ teaspoon ground nutmeg, divided
- ¼ teaspoon salt
- ¼ teaspoon pepper
- 2 tablespoons butter
- 1 tablespoon flour
- 1 cup beef broth
- 1 cup sour cream

Preparation:
1. In a large bowl combine the egg, meat, stuffing mix, ¼ teaspoon of the nutmeg and salt, and the pepper. Mix until well blended.
2. Shape into 1-inch meatballs.
3. Melt the butter in a large skillet on medium heat.
4. Add meatballs and cook until brown on all sides, stirring occasionally.
5. Remove meatballs from skillet and cover to keep warm.
6. Add flour to drippings in the skillet. And stir until well blended. Cook 1 Minute and add broth bring to boil. Reduce heat to low and simmer until thickened.
7. Stir in sour cream and remaining nutmeg.
8. Return meatballs to skillet and simmer until heated through.
9. Serve over noodles.

Touch of Italy Venison Meatballs

A simple recipe that produces awesome meatballs.

Serves: 8

Preparation Time: 10 Minutes

Cooking Time: 20 Minutes

Ingredients:
- 1 package stove top stuffing
- 2 pound ground venison
- 1¼ cups water
- 2 lightly beaten eggs
- 2 cloves garlic, minced
- ⅛ teaspoon pepper
- ⅓ cup grated parmesan cheese

Preparation:
1. Mix all ingredients in a large bowl until well blended.
2. Shape into meatballs.
3. Place in a single layer in a greased glass baking dish.
4. Bake at 400°F for 20 Minutes or until done.

Veggie and Barbeque Venison Meatballs

A little bit different way to prepare meatballs but yet very tasty.

Serves: 6

Preparation Time: 20 Minutes

Cooking Time: 60 Minutes

Ingredients:
- ½ cup Miracle Whip dressing
- ½ cup barbeque sauce
- ¼ cup honey
- 1 tablespoon chili powder, divided
- 1 teaspoon ground black pepper, divided
- 1 teaspoon cayenne pepper, divided
- 1 teaspoon salt
- 1 pound ground venison
- 1 green pepper, chopped
- 1 onion, chopped
- 1 cup mushrooms, sliced
- 1 cup yellow squash, chopped
- 1 cup zucchini, chopped
- 6 ounces drained pineapple chunks

Preparation:
1. In a bowl mix the dressing, barbeque sauce, honey, 2 teaspoons of the chili powder and ½ each of the peppers and salt. Set the mixture aside.
2. Mix the venison, remaining chili powder, peppers, and salt in a large bowl.
3. Shape mixture into 12 meatballs.
4. Brown meatballs in a large skillet.
5. Remove meatballs and set aside.
6. Drain grease from skillet and cook and stir the mixture of green pepper, onion, mushrooms, squash, zucchini and pineapple on medium heat for 10 Minutes.
7. Reduce heat to low and stir in the reserved dressing mixture and meatballs.
8. Cover and simmer for 20 Minutes.

Venison Meatball with Chipotle Sauce

Here's another take on meatballs that may become one of your favorites to serve at parties.

Serves: 20

Preparation Time: 15 Minutes

Cooking Time: 20 Minutes

Ingredients:
- 1 pound ground venison
- ¼ cup chopped cilantro
- 1 minced jalapeno pepper
- 1 egg, slightly beaten
- ¼ cup dry bread crumbs
- 3 cloves garlic, minced, divided
- ½ teaspoon salt
- ⅛ teaspoon black pepper
- 1 cup Mayonnaise
- 1 chipotle pepper in adobo sauce

Preparation:
1. Preheat the oven to 375°F.
2. Mix the venison, ciliantro, jalapeno, egg, bread crumbs, pepper and ⅔ of the garlic and salt until well blended.
3. Shape into 20 (1-inch) meatballs.
4. Place meatballs on a cookie sheet sprayed with cooking spray. Bake 20 Minutes or until meatballs are done.
5. Place the mayonnaise, remaining garlic and salt and chipotle pepper in a blender.
6. Blend until smooth and serve as a dip with the meatballs.

Venison Meatballs with a Picante Glaze

Appetizers prepared with a grape jelly and picante sauce are sure to surprise you.

Serves: 40

Preparation Time: 10 Minutes

Cooking Time: 35 Minutes

Ingredients:
- 1 pound ground venison
- ¼ cup dry bread crumbs
- 1 lightly beaten egg
- ⅛ teaspoon black pepper
- 3 cloves minced garlic
- 1 (16 ounce) jar Picante sauce
- ⅓ cup grape jelly
- 1 teaspoon thyme leaves

Preparation:
1. Heat the oven to 350°F.
2. In a large bowl mix the venison, bread crumbs, egg , pepper, garlic, and ¼ cup Picante sauce until well blended.
3. Shape the mixture into 40 (1-inch) meatballs.
4. Place the meatballs in a foil lined 15 x 10 inch baking pan. Bake for 15 Minutes or until done turning them over after 7½ Minutes.
5. Heat the remaining picante sauce and jelly and bring to a boil.
6. Reduce the heat to low, add the thyme and cook for 15 Minutes.
7. Add the meatballs to the skillet and cook until are hot.
8. Serve the meatballs on toothpicks.

Venison Salsa Meatballs

These meatballs are perfect for an everyday meal!

Serves: 4

Preparation Time: 15 Minutes

Cooking Time: 20 Minutes

Ingredients:
- 1¼ cups salsa
- 1½ pound ground venison
- 1 lightly beaten egg
- ¼ cup dry bread crumbs
- ¾ cup finely crushed tortilla chips
- ½ cup minced onions

Preparation:
1. Heat the oven to 350°F.
2. Thoroughly mix all the ingredients in a large bowl until well blended.
3. Shape the mixture into 16 meatballs.
4. Put the meatball into a 13x9x2 inch shallow baking dish.
5. Top each meatball with 1 teaspoon salsa.
6. Bake for 20 Minutes or until done.

Mac and Venison with a Tang

I've made this dish for years.

Serves: 4

Preparation Time: 5 Minutes

Cooking Time: 30 Minutes

Ingredients:
- 1 pound ground venison
- ⅛ teaspoon black pepper
- 1 (10 ounce) can condensed beef broth
- 1 cup water
- 2 cups uncooked shell shaped pasta
- 1 (10 ounce) can condensed cheddar cheese soup
- 1 cup picante sauce

Preparation:
1. In a skillet cook the venison over medium- high until well browned. Mix in the black pepper. Drain any grease.
2. Stir in the broth and water and bring to a boil. Stir in the pasta.
3. Reduce heat to medium and cook for 10 Minutes, stirring often.
4. Add the soup and picante sauce and stir until well blended.
5. Cook until the mixture is hot and bubbling.

Venison Party Treats

My absolute favorite way to eat venison. If you are making these at a party, be prepared to grill twice as many as you thought you would.

Serves: 6

Prep time: 15 Minutes

Cooking time: 8 Minutes

Ingredients:
- 1 pound venison chops or steaks
- 2 teaspoons Tony Chachere's Creole Seasoning
- ¾ teaspoon Chef Paul Prudhomme's Meat Magic
- ½ teaspoon garlic salt
- 1 tsp lemon pepper (optional)
- 4 tablespoon Worchestershire or Soy sauce
- 1 pound bacon
- Toothpicks

Preparation:
1. Cut venison into bite size pieces no thicker than 1 inch.
2. Mix all dry spices and sprinkle on meat to coat all sides evenly.
3. Place coated meat in a bowl and add Worchestershire sauce.
4. Mix to moisten all surfaces and press down so meat can marinate in the liquid.
5. Leave unrefrigerated for up to a couple of hours or it can be placed, covered in a refrigerator for a day or so.
6. Cut bacon into 3 inch strips and wrap each piece of venison , securing with a toothpick.
7. Grill at high heat no longer than 5 Minutes.
8. Turn once and grill for about another 3 Minutes.
9. Watch the flames from the bacon fat don't burn the bits too badly.

CAUTION: Remember to remove the toothpicks before eating. Sometimes the ends are burned off and you can't see them.

Chapter 6

Skillets

Gramma's Skillet Venison and Hash Browns

This was always one of my Dad's favorites.

Serves: 4

Preparation Time: 5 Minutes

Cooking Time: 25 Minutes

Ingredients:
- 1 pound ground venison
- 1 (10 ounce) can condensed cream of celery soup
- ½ cup water
- ¼ cup ketchup
- 1 tablespoon Worcestershire sauce
- 2 cups frozen hash brown potatoes
- Shredded cheddar cheese

Preparation:
1. Place the venison in a skillet and cook over medium heat until well browned, stirring often. Drain off any fat.
2. Stir in the soup, water, ketchup and Worcestershire sauce and bring to a boil. Stir in the potatoes.
3. Reduce the heat to low, cover and cook for 10 Minutes or until done.
4. Top with the cheddar cheese and serve.

Mushroom Venison Skillet Dinner

Try this recipe if you are looking for dinner in a hurry.

Serves: 4

Preparation Time: 5 Minutes

Cooking Time: 25 Minutes

Ingredients:
- 1 pound ground venison
- ½ cup chopped onion
- ¼ cup chopped green pepper
- 1 (10 ounce) can condensed mushroom soup
- 1 (10 ounce) can condensed beef broth
- 1/2 teaspoon crushed thyme leaves
- 1 (15 ounce) can diced tomatoes
- ½ cup sliced zucchini
- 1½ cup uncooked corkscrew-shaped pasta

Preparation:
1. Add the venison, onion, green pepper and garlic to a skillet over medium-high heat and stir until it is well blended and browned. Drain off any fat.
2. Add the soup, broth, thyme, tomatoes and zucchini.
3. Stir well and bring to a boil.
4. Stir in the pasta and reduce the heat to low and cook for 15 Minutes or until done.

New Mexico Venison Skillet

This terrific dish is another great way to use ground venison.

Serves: 6

Preparation Time: 10 Minutes

Cooking Time: 25 Minutes

Ingredients:
- 1 pound ground venison
- 2 teaspoons garlic, minced
- ¼ cup onion, chopped
- ¼ cup green peppers, chopped
- 1 tablespoon margarine
- 8 ounces Spanish rice
- 1 (15 ounce) can diced tomatoes
- ½ cup salsa
- 1 (15 ounce) can red kidney beans
- 1 (15 ounce) can whole kernel corn

Preparation:
1. In a large skillet brown the venison and stir in the onion , pepper and garlic until well blended.
2. Drain off fat and set the mixture aside in a bowl.
3. Melt the margarine in the skillet and stir in the rice and cook until done.
4. Add the cooked venison mixture, water, tomatoes, salsa and kidney beans. Stir until well blended and bring to a boil. Reduce heat to medium-low , cover and simmer for 15 Minutes.
5. Stir in corn and continue cooking another 5 Minutes or until done.

Pennsylvania Venison and Vegetable Skillet

One of my favorite dishes and it is easy to prepare.

Serves: 6

Preparation Time: 5 Minutes

Cooking Time: 15 Minutes

Ingredients:
- 1½ pound ground venison
- 2 (12 ounce) cans condensed tomato soup
- 3 teaspoons Worcestershire sauce
- 1 (16 ounce) bag frozen mixed vegetables
- 2 cups regular long-grain rice prepared to package directions
- Shredded Cheddar cheese

Preparation:
1. Cook the venison in a large skillet until well browned. Drain off any grease.
2. Add the soup, Worcestershire and vegetables to the skillet and stir.
3. Heat to a boil and reduce heat to low, stir and cook for 5 Minutes.
4. Serve the mixture over the rice and top with the cheese.

Rotini Skillet Venison and Vegetables

A great recipe using tasty venison ground meat.

Serves: 4

Preparation Time: 10 Minutes

Cooking Time: 30 Minutes

Ingredients:
- 1 pound ground venison
- ½ cup onion, chopped
- ⅛ teaspoon black pepper
- 1 teaspoon crushed dried basil leaves
- ½ teaspoon garlic powder
- 1 (10 ounce) can beef gravy
- 1 (10 ounce) bag frozen vegetables
- 2 cups rotini pasta cooked to package directions

Preparation:
1. Add the venison, onion, pepper, basil and garlic in a skillet and cook over medium –high heat until well blended and browned. Drain off any grease.
2. Add the gravy and vegetables and bring to a boil.
3. Reduce heat to low, cover and cook for 10 Minutes.
4. Stir in the rotini and cook until the mixture is hot and bubbling.

Skillet Picante Venison and Bean

You can't ask for an easier or more delicious meal.

Serves: 4

Preparation Time: 10 Minutes

Cooking Time: 20 Minutes

Ingredients:
- 1 pound ground venison
- 1 cup onion, chopped
- ½ cup chopped green pepper
- 1 (16 ounce) jar picante sauce
- 1 can drained red kidney beans
- 6 flour tortillas cut into pieces
- ½ cup shredded cheddar cheese

Preparation:
1. In a large skillet, add the venison, stir and heat until well browned. Drain any grease.
2. Stir in the remaining ingredients and bring to a boil.
3. Reduce the heat to low, stirring often and simmer until done.
4. Top with the cheese and serve.

Venison Enchiladas

The pay-off for preparing this meal will be well worth the effort.

Serves: 6

Preparation time: 15 Minutes

Cooking time: 20 Minutes

Ingredients:
- 1 pound ground venison
- 1 (16 ounce) jar picante sauce
- 2 cups shredded Cheddar cheese
- 12 corn or flour tortillas, warmed

Preparation:
1. Heat oven to 350°F.
2. Place the venison in a skillet over medium heat and stir until browned. Drain any fat.
3. Stir in ½ cup of picante sauce and 1 cup cheese.
4. Spread ½ cup picante sauce in a 3-quart baking dish.
5. Spoon about 2 tablespoons of venison mixture down the center of each tortilla.
6. Roll up and place seam-side down in the baking dish.
7. Top with the remaining picante sauce and cheese.
8. Bake for 20 minutes or until hot and the cheese melts.

Chapter 7

Soups and Stews

Winter Venison Stew in the Oven

You can't find a better way to use your stew meat.

Serves: 6

Preparation time: 20 Minutes

Cooking time: 2 Hours 15 Minutes

Ingredients:
- 8 tablespoons flour, divided
- ½ teaspoon salt, divided
- ½ teaspoon pepper, divided
- 1½ pounds venison stew meat
- 1 onion, chopped
- 1 tablespoon vegetable oil
- 2 cloves garlic, minced
- 3 cups beef broth
- 1 can diced tomatoes
- ½ teaspoon dried thyme
- 3 potatoes cut into 1 inch cubes
- 3 carrots, cut into ¼ inch slices
- ½ cup frozen peas, thawed

Preparation:
1. Add 4 tablespoons flour and half the salt and pepper in a large resealable bag. Add venison several pieces at a time and shake to coat.
2. Put vegetable oil in a Dutch oven and over medium-high heat add the coated venison in batches and brown. Remove browned venison and set aside.
3. Preheat the oven to 350° F.
4. Add onion to the pan and cook until tender. Add garlic and cook an additional minute.
5. Stir in the remaining flour, salt and pepper until well blended.
6. Stir in the beef broth. Add the venison, tomatoes and thyme. Cover and bake at 350° F for 1 Hour 15 Minutes.
7. Add the potatoes, carrots and peas. Cover and bake 1 Hour longer or until required doneness.

Venison Recipes Made Simple

George's Venison Stew

This recipe is just a great way to enjoy venison.

Serves: 6

Preparation time: 15 Minutes

Cooking time: 3 Hours 30 Minutes

Ingredients:
- 1 pound venison stew meat, cut into ½ inch pieces
- 1 onion, chopped
- 1 bag baby cut carrots
- 1 can diced tomatoes
- 1 can beef broth
- ⅓ cup all-purpose flour
- 1 tablespoon Worcestershire sauce
- 1 teaspoon salt
- 1 teaspoon sugar
- ½ teaspoon pepper
- 12 small red potatoes, cubed
- 1 can sliced mushrooms

Preparation:
1. Preheat oven to 325° F.
2. Mix all ingredients except potatoes and mushrooms in an oven-proof Dutch oven. Cover and bake for 2 Hours, stirring once.
3. Stir in the potatoes and mushrooms. Cover and bake 1 Hour and 30 Minutes longer or until required doneness.

Apple Venison Stew

Prepare this recipe and you will be pleased with the results.

Serves: 6

Preparation time: 20 Minutes

Cooking time: 4 Hours

Ingredients:
- 2 tablespoons butter
- 2 tablespoons olive oil
- 2 pound venison stew meat
- 4 onions, sliced
- 1 butternut squash, peeled seeded and cubed
- 6 apples, peeled and cubed
- 1 cup apple cider
- 3 cups maple syrup
- 4 teaspoon cinnamon

Preparation:
1. Melt butter in a skillet over medium heat and add olive oil.
2. Add venison and brown. Remove browned stew meat and place in a crockpot.
3. Layer the sliced onions on top of the venison, then add the butternut squash in a deep layer, and then add the apples.
4. Heat the cider to a boil in a pan and add the maple syrup, stirring.
5. Remove from the heat and stir in the spices.
6. Pour the mixture over the ingredients in the crockpot.
7. Cover and cook on high for 4 to 5 Hours or until required doneness.

Marinated Venison Stew

This family favorite has been around for a number of years.

Serves: 6

Preparation time: 15 Minutes

Cooking time: 8 Hours

Ingredients:
- 2 pound venison stew meat
- 1½ cups French dressing or Italian dressing
- 1 chopped green pepper
- 1 chopped onion
- 2 carrots, peeled and cut into ½ inch pieces
- 3 celery stocks, cut into ¾ inch pieces
- 1 can diced tomatoes
- ¼ cup quick cooking tapioca
- 1 garlic clove, minced
- ½ teaspoon salt
- ½ teaspoon pepper

Preparation:
1. Cut the venison into 1-inch cubes and place in a large resealable bag.
2. Pour the dressing over the venison and marinate in the refrigerator for 12 Hours.
3. Remove the venison from the bag and drain off excess dressing.
4. Put the venison in a crockpot with the other ingredients and stir until well blended.
5. Cook on low heat for 8 Hours.

Mr. Deans Ground Venison Soup

This recipe made me forget my Mom's bad preparation of venison.

Serves: 8

Preparation time: 20 Minutes

Cooking time: 2 Hours

Ingredients:
- 1 pound ground venison
- 1 large onion, chopped
- 1 cup celery, chopped
- 1 package dry onion soup mix
- 2 cups canned tomatoes
- 1 large potato, peeled and diced
- 1½ cups carrots, peeled and sliced
- 1 cup frozen peas
- 1 cup yellow squash, sliced

Preparation:
1. Brown venison in a large saucepan or Dutch oven with the onion and celery.
2. Add all other ingredients and mix well.
3. Cover and simmer for about 2 Hours or until vegetables are tender.

Don's Venison Vegetable Soup

I prefer this soup over store bought.

Serves: 8

Preparation time: 20 Minutes

Cooking time: 70 Minutes

Ingredients:
- ¾ pound venison, cubed
- 1 tablespoon vegetable oil
- 1 cup chopped onion
- 1 (16 ounce) frozen mixed vegetables
- 2 (14½ ounce) cans diced tomatoes
- 2 cups cubed peeled potatoes
- 2 cups water
- 1 tablespoon sugar
- 2 teaspoons beef bouillon granules
- 1 teaspoon salt
- ½ teaspoon pepper
- ½ teaspoon garlic powder
- ¼ teaspoon hot pepper sauce

Preparation:
1. Brown venison on all sides in oil in a Dutch oven or large saucepan.
2. Add onion and cover and simmer for 10 Minutes.
3. Add the remaining ingredients and cover and simmer 1 Hour longer or until required doneness.

Tasty Venison Cheese Ball Soup

A different yet tasty way to prepare a venison soup.

Serves: 8

Preparation time: 20 Minutes

Cooking time: 1 Hour 15 Minutes

Ingredients:
- 1 pound ground venison
- 1 tablespoon butter
- 1 onion, chopped
- 1 clove garlic, minced
- 1 (28 ounce) can whole tomatoes mashed
- 1 (18 ounce) can tomato juice
- 1 (15 ounce) can tomato sauce
- 1 (15 ounce) can pinto beans
- 1 tablespoon Worcestershire sauce
- 1 teaspoon basil
- ¼ teaspoon pepper
- 2 eggs, lightly beaten
- ½ cup grated parmesan cheese
- ½ cup finely rolled saltine cracker crumbs
- 4 cups shredded cabbage

Preparation:
1. In a large saucepan or Dutch oven, brown meat in butter and set aside to cool.
2. Place onion, garlic, tomatoes, juice, beans, Worcestershire sauce, basil and pepper in the pan.
3. Bring to a boil then cover and let simmer for 30 Minutes.
4. Combine eggs, parmesan, crackers and browned venison in a bowl.
5. Mix well and then shape into 1 Inch balls.
6. When soup has simmered 30 Minutes stir in cabbage and drop in venison cheese balls.
7. Cover and simmer an additional 30 Minutes.

Potato Venison Soup

This is a quick and easy way to make an awesome soup.

Serves: 8

Preparation time: 20 Minutes

Cooking time: 1 Hour

Ingredients:
- ½ pound ground venison
- 1 teaspoon butter
- 4 cups grated potatoes
- 1 chopped onion
- 1 (14½ ounce) can chicken broth
- 2 cups water
- 1 (10¾ ounce) can cream of celery soup
- 1 (10¾ ounce can) cream of chicken soup
- 2 cups milk
- 1½ teaspoon dried dill weed
- Shredded cheddar cheese for garnish

Preparation:
1. In a Dutch oven, brown venison in butter over medium heat.
2. Add potatoes, onion, chicken broth and water and heat to boiling.
3. Cover and reduce heat.
4. Simmer for 30 Minutes.
5. Add cream soups, milk and dill, stirring to blend.
6. Cook over medium heat for another 30 Minutes, stirring often.
7. Garnish with shredded cheddar cheese.

Chapter 8

Steaks

Country Fried Venison Steaks

This southern flavored recipe came from my nephew in Alabama.

Serves: 4

Preparation Time: 20 Minutes

Cooking Time: 4 to 8 Minutes

Ingredients:
- 2 pounds venison steaks or tenderloins
- 2 cups milk
- 2 teaspoons red pepper, divided
- 2 tablespoons black pepper, divided
- 2 teaspoons garlic salt, divided
- 1 egg, slightly beaten
- 1 teaspoon cornstarch
- 2 cups bread crumbs
- 1 cup vegetable oil

Preparation:
1. Mix the milk, half the red pepper, half the black pepper, half the garlic salt and the egg in a bowl.
2. Place the venison in the milk mixture.
3. Mix the remaining red pepper, black pepper and garlic salt with the cornstarch and bread crumbs in a shallow dish.
4. Add the vegetable oil to a skillet over medium heat.
5. Remove the venison from the milk mixture allowing the excess to run off, and press into the bread crumb mixture. Be sure to coat both sides thoroughly.
6. Drop the coated venison into the oil and cook for 2 to 3 Minutes per side until golden brown.

Venison Foil Packets on the Grill

This makes venison taste like it should.

Serves: 2

Preparation time: 10 Minutes

Cooking time: 10 Minutes

Ingredients:
- 1 pounds venison steak (¼ inch thick)
- 1 tablespoon butter
- 10 ounces mushrooms, sliced
- 1 medium onion, sliced
- 1 green pepper, sliced
- 1 teaspoon steak seasoning

Preparation:
1. Preheat the grill to medium high.
2. Place venison steak on foil.
3. Place butter on steak.
4. Cover steak with mushrooms, onion and green pepper.
5. Sprinkle steak seasoning over all.
6. Fold foil into packet and seal edges.
7. Place on hot grill for 10 Minutes flipping over at 5 Minutes.
8. Remove from grill and slice open being careful not to be burned by the hot steam.

Yummy Venison Steaks

If you enjoy venison, I know you'll love this recipe.

Serves: 4

Preparation time: 5 Minutes

Cooking time: 6 to 10 Minutes

Ingredients:
- 3 tablespoons butter
- 2 onions, sliced
- 2 garlic cloves, minced
- 1 green pepper, chopped
- 2 pounds venison steaks

Preparation:
1. Melt butter in a skillet over medium-high heat.
2. Add onions, garlic, and peppers and sauté.
3. Add venison and brown both sides.
4. Add ½ inch of water and cover with a lid.
5. Turn heat to medium-low and cook 6 to 10 Minutes or until done while maintaining water level.

Flour Coated Venison Steaks

The taste of these steaks is fantastic.

Serves: 4

Preparation time: 5 Minutes

Cooking time: 10 Minutes

Ingredients:
- 4 tablespoons flour
- 2 teaspoons Mrs. Dash® seasoning mix
- 1 teaspoon garlic salt
- 1 teaspoon onion salt
- 1 teaspoon black pepper
- 2 pounds venison steaks

Preparation:
1. Mix flour, seasoning mix, garlic salt, onion salt and black pepper together.
2. Coat both sides of venison steaks with the flour mixture.
3. Melt butter in a skillet over medium heat.
4. Add steaks to skillet and sauté for 10 Minutes or until done.

Broiled Marinated Venison Steaks

This is just another great way to enjoy venison.

Serves: 4

Preparation time: 10 Minutes

Cooking time: 8 Minutes

Ingredients:
- 4 (8 ounce) boneless venison steaks
- ½ cup white vinegar
- ½ cup ketchup
- ¼ cup vegetable oil
- ¼ cup Worcestershire sauce
- 2 tablespoons garlic salt
- 1 tablespoon ground mustard
- 1 teaspoon salt
- 1 teaspoon pepper

Preparation:
1. Place venison in a large Ziploc bag.
2. Combine all the other ingredients in a large bowl and mix well.
3. Pour half over the venison and seal bag.
4. Put the remaining marinade aside.
5. Refrigerate 6 to 12 Hours.
6. Drain and discard marinade from the steaks.
7. Broil steaks 3-4 inches from the heat for 4 Minutes.
8. Turn and baste with the reserved marinade.
9. Broil an additional 4 Minutes.

Grilled Venison Tenderloins

A basic venison recipe that I consider a classic.

Serves: 2

Preparation time: 10 Minutes

Cooking time: 6 Minutes

Ingredients:
- 4 venison tenderloins butterflied
- 1 cup Worcestershire sauce
- 2 cloves chopped garlic
- Salt
- Pepper

Preparation:
1. Put the Worcestershire sauce and garlic in a bowl and mix well.
2. Immerse each butterfly into the mixture coating both sides.
3. Remove and drain excess mixture.
4. Season with salt and pepper to taste.
5. Place venison on a hot grill and cook 3 Minutes per side or until required doneness.

Venison Steaks in the Oven or Crockpot

This is another quick meal for the busy person.

Serves: 4

Preparation time: 5 Minutes

Cooking time: 1 Hour

Ingredients:
- 4 venison steaks
- 1 can mushroom soup
- 6 teaspoons butter
- ½ cup milk
- 1 teaspoon salt
- 1 teaspoon pepper

Preparation:
1. Preheat oven to 350° F.
2. Put venison in large baking dish.
3. Combine all remaining ingredients in a bowl.
4. Pour mixture over venison.
5. Cover with foil and bake for 1 Hour or until required doneness.

NOTE: Instead of oven baking the recipe can be substituted using a crockpot set on low for 8 Hours.

Venison Chops and Rice in the Oven

A simple yet delicious solution to a last minute meal.

Serves: 4

Preparation time: 5 Minutes

Cooking time: 1 Hour

Ingredients:
- 4 venison chops
- 4 tablespoons uncooked rice
- 4 slices onion
- 4 slices tomato
- 4 slices bell pepper
- 1 can chicken broth

Preparation:
1. Brown the chops on both sides.
2. Preheat the oven at 350°F.
3. Grease a baking dish.
4. Put one tablespoon of rice per chop into the bottom of the dish.
5. Place each chop on a rice pile.
6. Cover each chop with a slice of onion, tomato and pepper.
7. Cover the entire dish with the can of chicken broth.
8. Bake at 350°F for 1 Hour or until required doneness.

Perfect Venison Steaks on the Grill

The name of this recipe describes the steaks you can expect.

Serves: 4

Preparation time: 10 Minutes

Cooking time: 6 Minutes

Ingredients:
- 2 pounds venison steaks
- 1 bottle Italian dressing
- ¼ cup red wine vinegar
- 1 tablespoon olive oil
- 2 tablespoons fresh basil, chopped
- 1 clove garlic, chopped
- 1 teaspoon salt
- 1 teaspoon black pepper

Preparation:
1. Tenderize the steaks with a mallet.
2. Place the steaks into a large Ziploc bag.
3. Combine the salad dressing with the other ingredients and pour over the steaks.
4. Seal bag and make sure the marinade contacts every surface.
5. Marinate the venison steaks for 12 to 24 Hours in the refrigerator before grilling.
6. Preheat the grill to medium high heat and cook for 2 to 3 Minutes each side or until required doneness.

Chapter 9

Jerky

Tried and True Venison Jerky

This is a very basic method to make jerky.

Only Oven Needed

Ingredients:
- 1 teaspoon onion powder
- 1 teaspoon black pepper
- 1 teaspoon garlic powder
- 1 tablespoon salt
- ¼ cup soy sauce
- ⅓ cup Worcestershire sauce
- 3 pounds venison cut into ½" x ¼" inch thick strips

Preparation:
1. Mix all of the above ingredients and pour over meat. Marinate overnight in refrigerator (minimum of 8 Hours for best results) in a sealed bags.
2. Preheat oven to 200°.
3. Place meat on baking sheets and cook for about 3 to 5 Hours or until completely dry.
4. Store jerky in airtight containers or plastic bags.

Sweet and Zesty Venison Jerky

This is a great way to use up venison you have left in the freezer.

Food Dehydrator Needed

Ingredients:
- 1 tablespoon black pepper
- 1 tablespoon onion power
- 1 tablespoon garlic salt
- 1 teaspoon paprika
- 1 tablespoon lemon juice
- 1 teaspoon hot pepper sauce
- 2 tablespoons liquid smoke flavoring
- ½ cup Worcestershire sauce
- ⅓ cup soy sauce
- 1 pound venison cut into ¼ inch thick strips

Directions:
1. In a large bowl, mix together all of the ingredients except for the venison.
2. Add in the venison strips and cost with mixture evenly. Cover bowl and place in refrigerator for at least 24 Hours. For best results, be sure to mix the meat and mixture a few times while marinating.
3. Remove from mixture and remove any excess liquid. Be sure to discard the liquid.
4. Arrange strips on the racks and ensure no overlap.
5. Dry the venison on high for about 4 Hours or until dry. The jerky should bend but not break in two.
6. Store jerky in airtight containers or resalable plastic bags.

All Ground Venison Jerky

This terrific recipe uses ground venison to make some great jerky.

Only Oven Needed

Ingredients:
- 2 pounds ground venison
- 1 tablespoon Morton's Tender Quick© salt
- 3 tablespoons table salt
- ½ tablespoon black pepper
- ½ tablespoon garlic powder
- ½ tablespoon cayenne powder
- 2 teaspoons cardamom
- ½ ounce liquid smoke flavoring
- ½ ounce water

Directions:
1. Preheat oven to 200°F or lowest setting on your oven.
2. Mix together venison, quick salt, table salt, pepper, garlic powder, cayenne and cardamom in a large bowl.
3. Place meat mixture between sheets of waxed paper and roll until ¼ inch thick.
4. Mix in small bowl liquid smoke and water. Brush onto rolled meat mixture.
5. Place meat on baking tray in oven and cook for 3 to 4 Hours or until dry.
6. Once meat is dry and cooled, cut into strips of your desired size.
7. Store jerky in airtight containers or resalable plastic bags.

A Bit of Kick Venison Jerky

People will think you used a smoker to prepare this jerky.

Only Oven Needed

Ingredients:
- ½ teaspoon salt
- ½ teaspoon pepper
- ½ teaspoon garlic powder
- ½ teaspoon onion powder
- 1 teaspoon liquid smoke
- ¼ cup soy sauce
- 1 tablespoon A-1 Steak Sauce©
- 1 tablespoon Worcestershire sauce
- 1½ pound venison cut into ⅛ inch thick strips

Directions:
1. In a large bowl, mix together all of the ingredients except for the venison.
2. Add in the venison strips and cost with mixture evenly. Cover bowl and place in refrigerator for at least 12 Hours. For best results, be sure to mix the meat and mixture a few times while marinating.
3. The next day, Preheat oven to 200°F or lowest setting on your oven.
4. Remove strips from the marinade, rinse off under water and pat dry with paper towels.
5. Place meat on baking tray in oven and cook for 3 to 4 Hours or until dry.
6. Store jerky in airtight containers or plastic bags.

Index

Made in United States
Cleveland, OH
04 December 2024

11320209R00070